Greater Than a Tourist
Book Series
Reviews from Readers

I think the series is wonderful and beneficial for tourists to get information before visiting the city.

-Seckin Zumbul, Izmir Turkey

I am a world traveler who has read many trip guides but this one really made a difference for me. I would call it a heartfelt creation of a local guide expert instead of just a guide.

-Susy, Isla Holbox, Mexico

New to the area like me, this is a must have!

 -Joe, Bloomington, USA

This is a good series that gets down to it when looking for things to do at your destination without having to read a novel for just a few ideas.

-Rachel, Monterey, USA

Good information to have to plan my trip to this destination.

-Pennie Farrell, Mexico

Great ideas for a port day.

-Mary Martin USA

Aptly titled, you won't just be a tourist after reading this book. You'll be greater than a tourist!

-Alan Warner, Grand Rapids, USA

Even though I only have three days to spend in San Miguel in an upcoming visit, I will use the author's suggestions to guide some of my time there. An easy read - with chapters named to guide me in directions I want to go.

 -Robert Catapano, USA

Great insights from a local perspective! Useful information and a very good value!

 -Sarah, USA

This series provides an in-depth experience through the eyes of a local. Reading these series will help you to travel the city in with confidence and it'll make your journey a unique one.

-Andrew Teoh, Ipoh, Malaysia

GREATER THAN A TOURIST- LONG ISLAND NEW YORK USA

50 Travel Tips from a Local

Elizabeth Macrelli

First Edition
Cover designed by: Ivana Stamenkovic
Cover Image: By King of Hearts - Own work, CC BY-SA 4.0,
https://commons.wikimedia.org/w/index.php?curid=63514051

Image 1: By United States Coast Guard, photo by Pamela Bednarik - U.S. Coast Guard
photo ID 080817-G-0000X-015Photo page: [1]Photo description page: [2]U.S. Coast Guard
Visual Information Gallery [3], Public Domain,
https://commons.wikimedia.org/w/index.php?curid=8016820
Image 2: By Kelvinsong - Own work, CC0,
https://commons.wikimedia.org/w/index.php?curid=22858627
Image 3: By Jsayre64 - Own work, CC BY-SA 3.0,
https://commons.wikimedia.org/w/index.php?curid=27898189
Image 4: By AdmOxalate - Own work, CC BY 3.0,
https://commons.wikimedia.org/w/index.php?curid=7711855
Editing Suggestions by Donna Ballard-
Reader Services Librian at Eat Meadow Public Library

CZYK Publishing Since 2011.

Greater Than a Tourist
Lock Haven, PA
All rights reserved.

ISBN: 9798697273951

>TOURIST

50 TRAVEL TIPS FROM A LOCAL

BOOK DESCRIPTION

With travel tips and culture in our guidebooks written by a local, it is never too late to visit Long Island. Greater Than a Tourist- Long Island, New York by Author Elizabeth Macrelli offers the inside scoop on The Year-Round Island. Most travel books tell you how to travel like a tourist. Although there is nothing wrong with that, as part of the 'Greater Than a Tourist' series, this book will give you candid travel tips from someone who has lived at your next travel destination. This guide book will not tell you exact addresses or store hours but instead gives you knowledge that you may not find in other smaller print travel books. Experience cultural, culinary delights, and attractions with the guidance of a Local. Slow down and get to know the people with this invaluable guide. By the time you finish this book, you will be eager and prepared to discover new activities at your next travel destination.

Inside this travel guide book you will find:

Visitor information from a Local
Tour ideas and inspiration
Save time with valuable guidebook information

Greater Than a Tourist- A Travel Guidebook with 50 Travel Tips from a Local. Slow down, stay in one place, and get to know the people and culture. By the time you finish this book, you will be eager and prepared to travel to your next destination.

OUR STORY

Traveling is a passion of the Greater than a Tourist book series creator. Lisa studied abroad in college, and for their honeymoon Lisa and her husband toured Europe. During her travels to Malta, an older man tried to give her some advice based on his own experience living on the island since he was a young boy. She was not sure if she should talk to the stranger but was interested in his advice. When traveling to some places she was wary to talk to locals because she was afraid that they weren't being genuine. Through her travels, Lisa learned how much locals had to share with tourists. Lisa created the Greater Than a Tourist book series to help connect people with locals. A topic that locals are very passionate about sharing.

TABLE OF CONTENTS

DEDICATION

This book is dedicated to my amazing parents, with all their love and support, and I wouldn't have pursued my dreams.

ABOUT THE AUTHOR

Elizabeth is a writer who lives in Islip, New York, a little beach town on the south shore of Long Island. She loves to read about true crime and spend time with her large Italian family.

HOW TO USE THIS BOOK

The *Greater Than a Tourist* book series was written by someone who has lived in an area for over three months. The goal of this book is to help travelers either dream or experience different locations by providing opinions from a local. The author has made suggestions based on their own experiences. Please check before traveling to the area in case the suggested places are unavailable.

Travel Advisories: As a first step in planning any trip abroad, check the Travel Advisories for your intended destination.
https://travel.state.gov/content/travel/en/traveladvisories/traveladvisories.html

FROM THE PUBLISHER

Traveling can be one of the most important parts of a person's life. The anticipation and memories that you have are some of the best. As a publisher of the Greater Than a Tourist, as well as the popular *50 Things to Know* book series, we strive to help you learn about new places, spark your imagination, and inspire you. Wherever you are and whatever you do I wish you safe, fun, and inspiring travel.

Lisa Rusczyk Ed. D.
CZYK Publishing

WELCOME TO
> TOURIST

Montauk Point is at Long Island's rural eastern tip

The bluffs of the North Shore

Cumulus congestus clouds over Long Island on a summer afternoon

Photograph of CSHL (Cold Spring Harbor Laboratory) in the fall of 2008

*"The world is full of magic
things, patiently waiting for our
sense to grow sharper"*

W.B Yeats.

L ong Island has been my home since the beginning; I have lived in Islip, New York, most of my life. Islip is a small beach town located in the southern, central Long Island. Islip is up against sandy beaches, that leads to the slaty waters of the bay. This small, boutique town has a little mom and pop shops and formal and casual restaurants.

South from Upstate New York and east of New York City, Long Island is a combination of massive roads, towns, and numerous activities available to experience. The Long Island Sound sandwiches in the Island on its northern side, the Atlantic Ocean is on the eastern point of the island, the New York Bay and East River on its west side, and finally the Great South Bay on the island's southern side. In other words, Long Island is an actual island.

Long Island consists of four counties; two counties are considered part of the five boroughs, Queens and

Brooklyn. Nassau (west part of the island) and Suffolk (eastern part of the island) are the bulk of the island. They comprise of suburban towns and beaches.

The island is one of the most memorable vacation spots in America. There is so much to do in the 118.1 miles of the Island. Long Island is a year-round full of fun designation that everyone needs to experience. Long Island has so many activities all year round that everyone should share; beaches, apple picking, pumpkin picking, the change of the leaves, holiday parades and light shows, and beautiful state parks to explore. Of course, there is much more!

In this tips and tricks tourist book, I will introduce the treasures and most visited places on Long Island. I will also offer tips and tricks on navigating your way to make sure the experience is comfortable. Make sure that your next fun trip with the family is on Long Island.

Long Island
New York, USA

Long Island New York Climate

	High	Low
January	41	24
February	43	25
March	49	31
April	61	41
May	70	51
June	79	60
July	84	67
August	83	66
September	77	60
October	67	49
November	56	38
December	47	31

GreaterThanaTourist.com

Temperatures are in Fahrenheit degrees.
Source: NOAA

1. THE TREASURE OF LONG ISLAND: THE BEACHES

As you all probably guessed, one of the most popular places to see on the island is the gorgeous beaches. Because of the smoothness of the sand, the southern part of the island is more ideal for beachgoers. The north side beaches are made up of rocks. A few of the favorite spots are Jonas Beach, the home of the Jonas Beach Theater, and Robert Moses. Both of these beaches you can drive to. They are easy to get to and have plenty of parking, but you want to get there early. There will be no areas to lay your beach towel down near the shore if you go anywhere past noon. You should get there either mid-morning or early morning. Also, pack a lunch, if you are able too; it will save you money. The concession stands most feel is too expensive.

2. FIRE ISLAND

Fire Island is a little strip of land that is on the southern side of Long Island. It's is all by itself, only connected to the mainland by bridges. Fire Island is most popular in the summertime because of the shops, beaches, and yummy restaurants. There are a few locals that do stay on the island all year round. These homeowners rely on the few markets and restaurants that remain open. Fire Island is one of the most visited locations of Long Island during the summer. This tiny island consists of fourteen villages. Most of the villages are only accessible through the ferries, and the towns don't allow personal cars. So, make sure to bring your bike or scooter to get around. There are plenty of bike rental shops that do daily or weekly rentals, depending on how long you're expected to stay. Each town is lined with little beach looking homes that are all named by their owners. A few of my favorites are located in Ocean Beach. For example, 'The Reel World, Victoria's Sea-Crest,' 'Loony Dunes,' and 'Coconut Cottage.' All of the houses have their names presented by the front door or fence.

3. OCEAN BEACH

Ocean Beach is the central location of Fire Island. It is the most famous town on the barrier island. It houses the most all-year-round homeowners, nicknamed OB, offers bed and breakfasts, and hotels if you can't find a rental cottage. Each home usually has multiple bedrooms; some have twin beds or bunk beds for larger families. They all have kitchens and back patios with furniture to lounge around on. Kismet is another fun place to visit on Fire Island. Mostly famous for its beaches, Kismet is walking distance from the Fire Island Lighthouse. Not many towns on Fire Island are assessable by driving or walking, but Kismet is. A lot of the villages on Fire Island are primarily assessable by ferry.

Kismet has a few Inn's, or you can rent a cottage beach house. Many of them are on the water or walking distance to the beach. Of course, this little beach town has a lot of tasty and fun places to hang out. When traveling to Fire Island, like Ocean Beach, take the ferry out of Bay Shore. Bay Shore is a little southern central town on Long Island. Two boats leave from Bay Shore. Ocean Beach and Ocean Bay Park. From that ferry, Ocean Beach, Ocean Bay, and

Seaview are all walking distance from each other. The only ports back to the mainland, though is from Ocean Beach and Ocean Bay Park.

4. SHOPPING ON OCEAN BEACH

Be sure to visit the boutiques that line along main street in Ocean Beach; for example, Oh La La. Oh, La La is a chic women's clothing store that sells unique items that you won't find anywhere else. They are the kind of store where they only have a few pieces of one thing. If you don't grab it when you see it, when you come back, it will be gone. Another popular store is Bambootique. They sell a lot of Vans, Vineyard Vines, and Obey type clothing. From Sweatshirts, t-shirts, bathing suits, bathing suit cover-ups, etc., they have a wide variety for everyone. This is also a great place to buy some souvenirs for your family, friends, or maybe yourself. Kismet is on the smaller side than the rest of the towns on fire island, but it has the most beautiful beaches, boardwalks, and fantastic foods. There isn't much shopping in Kismet, but there are surrounding towns that offer more.

5. THE BAY SHORE FERRY

Bay Shore Ferry has multiple ports depending on what part of Fire Island you are traveling from. The ferry everyone usually gets on is the ferry to Ocean Beach. Other locals and visitors head towards the Ocean Bay Park Ferry Port and the Seaview Ferry Port. There is also water taxi's available to take you to locations that don't have a ferry port or driving accessible like Point of Woods and Cherry Grove. A tip if you are driving your vehicle to the ferry ports, there is parking, but it fills up fast. The town of Bay Shore doesn't have ample parking lots, and the ones you find you will have to pay. Take the train in. Depending on where you are staying, you can jump on the Long Island Railroad and take it to Bay Shore. From there, you walk down a few blocks, and you will see the ferry ports. This will save you money and be a stress-free way to get to paradise. If you have a lot of stuff you are bringing, you may want to park near the ferry. It is a few blocks, and you have to cross a major road.

6. RULES OF THE FIRE ISLAND TOWNS AND BEACHES

Fire Island beaches have strict rules! You need to follow them, or you'll end up with a fine. Each town and its corresponding beach all have limitations. The most important rule that most of the beaches have is no food on the beaches. Do not pack a lunch or bring take out. You will be asked to leave and then fined. Fire Island is praised for its well-kept beaches. You want to avoid this cost! There are many other little rules in each town that you need to follow, like ringing your bike bell when coming to an intersection. Since there are no cars, your only other transportation is bikes and scooters. No matter where you rent your "vehicles" from, they are all equipped with bells. This is put in place to avoid accidents. Since there are no traffic lights or stop signs, they put in the bell rule for this reason. If you are caught flying through an intersection, you could be pulled over and written a fine. Yes! This does happen! And it mostly happens to out of towners. Be careful! All rules are usually on some sort of a sign as you get off the ferry or get closer to the beach.

7. LOCAL EATING ON FIRE ISLAND

When eating local, there are so many unique places to eat on the island. There are plenty of places to eat on Ocean Beach. One of my favorites is Rachel's Bakery. If you are looking for a fantastic breakfast or brunch place, Rachel's got you! It is a little hole in the wall location right in Ocean Beach Town. Rachel's was founded in 1975; Rachels Bakery started as a small bakery. They were only selling a few classic items, like chocolate chip cookies and Black Magic cake. In 1990 the tiny bakery expanded to include a full restaurant. This is a staple restaurant of fire island. Anyone who stays in Ocean Beach usually finds their way to Rachel's for breakfast or an early lunch. Fun Fact about Rachel's: long ago, you were not allowed to eat on the streets of ocean beach. The sidewalks banned people from wearing while exploring the other locations in town. But Rachel's fought hard to abolish that law, which they did! Now you are welcomed to walk down the sidewalks in town with one of her amazing cookies and muffins. Another fun fact, Rachel has passed the torch over to her kids after 43 years of running it herself with the help of her staff and spouse. Since 2018, her son and daughter, Joe Doering and Pam Grehan, with their spouses, Angela Doering and Kevin Grehan, have been running it, and they are holding their mother's legacy very well.

Another staple of Ocean Beach is Maguire's Bayfront Restaurant. This restaurant is one of the most prime stops in Ocean Beach. They have indoor dining, but why would you want to do that when they have an enormous deck overlooking the bay. They have the most incredible view of the water, boats passing, and the incoming ferries. Their most astounding beauty is the sunset. You want to make sure that you go around then to see the sky change colors as the sun dips into the sky behind the mainland of Long Island. You won't regret it. From Short Ribs to King Crab legs, they have the tastiest dinner and lunch menus. They also make killer drinks. They offer wine, beer, and fun cocktails like The Fire Island Mule, to The Zippy. Be sure to visit this fantastic and unique restaurant on the island.

8. LOCAL EATING ON EASTERN LONG ISLAND

Lucharitos has to be the most famous American/Mexican restaurant in Greenport. They are so popular, and they opened a "Little" Lucharitos in Riverhead to keep up with demand. It doesn't matter what time you show up to this colorful restaurant in the summertime; there is always a wait to get in. This Taqueria and Tequila Bar is to die for! Their food is fresh and amazing to eat, but even better, their margaritas are addicting. All of their ingredients, even with their drinks, are fresh and well thought out. Be warned, and they are only open fully in the summer months; After the holidays, they are only opened for the weekend.

9. EASTERN LONG ISLAND

Most people, when they come to visit Long Island, they all turn to eastern Long Island for their vacation fun. From Riverhead and to Montauk, welcomes millions of tourists each year. Sometimes you will see celebrities walking the streets of East Hampton or

Greenport. People have seen Jerry Seinfeld driving one of his expensive cars, Jimmy Fallon walking with his kids and wife, and even Paul McCartney out and enjoying ice cream on a hot summer day. The Kardashians are another well-known family to be seen in the Hamptons; their homes can be found on Dune Road in the Hampton Bays area.

The eastern part of the island is very different than in the middle of the island. The island becomes narrower as you get closer to the end. There are no significant highways on the most eastern part of the island; most of the roads you will be driving on our local residential roads or "Main Street." The Long Island Expressway ends in Riverhead. From there, it becomes all local streets with lights. There is a lot of traffic in the eastern area of Long Island. Since there is no major highway, locals and tourists rely on these main roads that have stop signs and stoplights to get to their dentation. Or you could be stuck behind a tractor.

The eastern part of the island is mostly farmland and wineries. The new thing popping up in the east end are breweries. They are wildly popular among the younger crowd. A lot of them offer outside seating, and you're welcomed to bring your dog along for a good day. The local wineries are pretty sort after too. You will see many bachelorette parties traveling in party busses and limos enjoying the local wine and beautiful outdoor seating. Some of the wineries offer food, but most of them allow you to bring your own. Breweries provide food, but it's mostly pub food; for example, wings, tacos, and soft pretzels. Farmland on the east end usually has a stand where you can purchase their fruits and vegetables. Many people from all over the island travel to the farm stand to pick up their weekly haul of vegetables and fruit. For some reason, the veggies and fruits taste better when they come straight from the farmer, and I am not sure why.

As the seasons' change, so does the eastern part of the island. They go from a beach and summer fun to an apple picking, pumpkin picking, candy apples, corn mazes in a blink of an eye. If you think summer is popular out there, you have never experienced a fall season on Long Island—everyone flocks to the farm stands, pumpkin patches, and apple picking trees. I feel the traffic is worst at this time of the year. Breweries start to offer apple cider, and large heaters are put along the perimeter of the outdoor seating to keep their customers warm when dining. The transition is pretty flawless.

10. DUNE ROAD

It is a good thing that Dune Road's speed limit is only 30 miles per hour because you need to see the houses. Located in Hamptons, this 14-mile road has some of the most beautiful homes. These are beach mansions that overlook the water. Celebrities occupy most of these homes, for example, New York Giants former quarterback, Eli Manning, soap opera stars, Susan Lucci, and magazine editor Tina Brown. This is a must-see. The homes are not only gorgeous, but the surroundings are even more memorable. When you get to the end of the road, you'll come to a restaurant, Sunday's On the Bay, which is a fantastic place to stop and grab a bite to eat. You will also see a small beach that you can spend the rest of your day in front of the ocean. Be sure to check for paid parking signs or permit only signs; you can receive a ticket or be towed.

11. THE DIFFERENCE BETWEEN THE NORTH FORK AND THE SOUTH FORK

The eastern part of the island splits into two forks at the end; the North Fork and the South Fork. Both are entirely different. The North Fork is the more rustic or known as the "un-Hampton" side of the island. The South Fork is a lot quieter; it is meant for sunbathers who want to spend their day at a calm beach. The north side has many more to do, wineries, breweries, farm stands, and boutique shops. The beaches aren't as famous on the north side due to the rocky shores, but with all the activities going on all summer and fall, you won't have time to miss it. The North and South both have points to them, but Orient Point on the Northside is not as popular as Montauk Point. Orient Point is the end of the island but doesn't offer much. You could always hop the Orient Point Ferry to New London, Connecticut. Taking the ferry over, you can access I-95 North and continue into New England and the Connecticut casinos. The ferry allows walk on's and drive on vehicles. It is an hour and a twenty-five-minute ride.

12. THE NORTH FORK

The North Fork has a few little towns for the best shopping and fun, and Greenport is one. Greenport is a trendy hangout for anyone trying to get away from reality. Right on a harbor, you can enjoy the sights of sag harbor across the channel and the luxurious yachts, and sometimes ships docked along the boardwalk. A few small shops to see, such as Burton's Books, The Times Vintage, and Crinoline Fashion Boutique. There is also Mitchell's Park Carousel; it is a 100-year-old carousel that is still working today. It is strangely sat in the middle of the grass overlooking the channel and the boats. It is super fun, and your kids will enjoy it.

If you are visiting Long Island with your kids, you want to take them to Harbes Family Farms. They have multiple locations on the north fork. All of them have different purposes, depending on the season. They all have various events happening, such as apple picking, watermelon picking, peach harvests, etc. They are one of the largest farms out on the North Fork and offer so much fun for the kids. They have playgrounds and other activities to keep the kids busy all day. Just a few of their locations include Harbes Barnyard, Harbes Orchard, Harbes Farms, etc. They offer all-year-round fun for families.

13. SAG HARBOR FERRY

Since the forks are separated by a body of water, to get to the other fork, you can hop a ride onto the Sag Harbor drive on ferry. You can catch the ferry in Greenport or Sag Harbor. It all depends on what fork you're on and need to get too. Sag Harbor is a hamlet of East Hampton and one of the most popular southern fork town. This will save time, gas, and wear and tear on your vehicle. Driving from one fork to the other can be tedious, especially during the summer. Summer and Fall are the busiest times for the east end of Long Island. You want to avoid it as much as possible.

14. SOUTH FORK

East Hampton is one of the most visited areas of the south fork other than Montauk. This little town is home to many and has many visitors because of its luxurious shopping. These stores are high end, super chic looking pieces of clothing that you won't be able to find anywhere else. Depending on your style, there are different shops for different looks. There are also art galleries to buy paintings from local artists, household decorating stores, book shops, and a vinyl shop. You need to stop in a few of these stores. Many of these stores are pop-ups; what that means in East Hampton is that many of the shops stay for the summer and fall season, and during the winter months, when it is quiet, another brand will take over for the following summer.

15. PRIVATE BEACHES

You want to be super careful about what beach you're going to on the forks. You want to check out the rules of the beach you want to spend the day at. Many of these houses are privately owned, meaning families live on the forks all year round. A lot of these homeowners also own the beachfront as well. There are many rentals beachfront homes as well, but you need to be sure. The homeowner has the right to call the police for anyone "trespassing" on their property. But don't fear, many the owners have spent many summers in their home and know that sometimes, the signs aren't clear. They will come down and kindly ask you to leave. Others don't mind the company. It all depends on who owns the home. Usually, where you park indicated if it is a private beach or a public beach.

16. SHOP LOCAL ON THE SOUTH FORK

This is Gwyneth Paltrow's lifestyle brand, Goop. Goop is a pop-up type shop. The brand usually stays for the summer and is gone before the leaves change color. She offers her favorite fashion, wellness items, home, and beauty products. They also host cocktail parties, wellness workshops, and events for families. LoveShackFrancy brand converted a 1970's farmhouse into a retail store. On Main Street in Sag Harbor (a hamlet of East Hampton,) you will find this chic little shop. This is a luxury lifestyle brand that you won't find anywhere else. This location is beautifully decorated with soft florals and soft music to help your shopping experience comfortable and relaxed. The brand's collection includes custom sweaters from Lingua Franca, saris from India, sandals from Loeffler Randall, and bags from Morocco from the namesake brand that combines, LoveShackFancy and the United Nations Ethical Fashion Initiative.

Love Adorned is a well-collected inventory of fine jewelry and one of a kind pieces that have been created by Loir Leven. The pieces that her travels across Amagansett inspired her. You want to head to Love, Adorned if you are looking for one of a kind gifts for your loved ones. Or maybe you're looking to get married, their engagement rings are handmade, and you won't find anything like it in a chain store like Kay or Jared. Love, Adorned also has clothing made by Mara Hoffman; her collection is of swimsuits, dresses, etc. Personally, this is probably my favorite store on the south fork of Long Island. This bookstore is bright, spaced out, and has the cutest gifts. But of course, you're there to buy a book. They have the floor to ceiling shelves of books. They have the books separated into genres, bestsellers, and the store staff picks. Book Hampton also has small gifts, like specialty pens, pencil cases, cute totes with book quotes on them, etc. They are my favorite bookstore to visit when I am looking for my new page-turner.

17. EAT LOCAL ON THE SOUTH FORK

Suppose you are looking for high-quality seafood with a casual atmosphere, head over to Bostwick's Chowder House. They have been around for 18 years, serving the visitors and locals of east Hampton their very best seafood dishes. Bostwick's has a laid back, casual experience. The owners, Chris Eggert, and Kevin Boles established this fresh eatery for the sole purpose for locals to have a friendly and comfortable environment. Chris is the head chef, prepares the fresh catch of the day while Kevin creates new cocktails; both owners are very involved. Bostwick's offers outdoor and indoor dining, take out, a full bar, ice cream, and their very own merchandise.

18. WINERIES ON EASTERN LONG ISLAND

Pindar is one of the largest wineries that offers so much for its customers. Their grounds are enormous for any events going on. They provide deck seating; lawn seating, and they even have an open pavilion. Pindar invites different food trucks on their campus due to their lack of food available. They have one of the most tasting rooms, with a large wrap-around bar and individual seating scattered around the open floor. The staff is knowledgeable, kind, and offer the best customer service. You'll be leaving with several bottles of their tasty wines.

Macari is a famous winery on the north fork of the eastern end of Long Island. They are a high-end quality winery that offers tastings and full glass orders. Macari also sells their wine bottles to take home. Be sure to join their wine club; they have some great perks for their members, such as 20% off all wine orders, access to new releases, and Admission to an annual wine dinner hosted by the Macari family. The perks also depend on what level of the wine club you are in. They offer outdoor and indoor seating, but

when you see the grounds, you will want to stay
outside enjoying the view.

19. GREENPORT HARBOR BREWERY

Greenport Harbor Brewery. The Greenport
Brewery is not in town, but pretty close to it. They
have an indoor area where they have bands and places
to sit to enjoy their refreshing taps. But what makes it
worth the time and money spent in the outdoor space.
Covered in lawn chairs, picnic tables, and lawn
games, this area is everything! Relax in the sun with a
flight while listening to one of their best Blue Grass
bands that they invite to play every week. One of the
most popular events they offer is the Dog Jumping
Contest. Dogs from all over the island and the New
England area are welcome to show off their jumping
skills. Of course, these puppies are jumping off a
platform and into the water, so don't worry, they
won't hurt themselves. It is usually a two-day event at
the beginning of June to kick off their summer
season. They also off some yummy tacos, empanadas,

and giant soft pretzels to soak up all that beer. Be sure
to get their early because they have a tiny parking lot.

20. FIRE ISLAND LIGHTHOUSE HISTORY

The Fire Island Lighthouse is one of the most
historic places on Long Island. This landmark
attraction pulls in a lot of tourists. They offer tours
and history lessons about the lighthouse; also, you
can climb the steep, narrow, spiral staircase to the top.
From the top, you can look over Fire Island and parts
of Long Island. Be sure to get your memorable
photos from the top! Especially if you go around
when the sunsets. It is an exceptionally professional
magazine cover-worthy! The lighthouse was an
important landmark for transatlantic ships coming
into New York Harbor during the last century. For
European immigrants, the Fire Island Lighthouse was
their first sight of America. It was their first sight of
freedom and new land.

When they first build the lighthouse in 1826, it
was 74-feet and made of Connecticut River bluestone.
It was painted a cream color. It was built at the end of

the inlet as close to the water as possible, but it was hardly seen due to it not being tall enough. Today, there is just a ring of brick, left of the old lighthouse, and a few yards away is the lighthouse that stands today. In 1857, congress approved funding of $400,000 to build a new lighthouse. This one was going to be built at 168 feet tall. And for the first time, on November 1st, 1858, the light was lit. The current tower is made of red brick and striped black and cream colors. The stripes were not added until August 1891. The building was fitted with the First Order Fresnel Lens; this allows a white flash to appear in one-minute intervals. As the years went on, fuels to light the lamp has changed over the years, for example, whale oil, lard oil, mineral oil, and kerosene. Not until September 20th, 1938, electricity was welcomed to the lighthouse. But, the next day, September 21st, 1938, a hurricane hit the island and cut the electricity causing a power outage throughout the island.

Between 1974-1980, people fought to save the lighthouse; as time went on, the lighthouse had become obsolete, but the historic nature was there. But they were able to keep it and made it part of Robert Moses Beach State Park. Because of a

Preservation Society, the lighthouse is protected and maintained by people who believe in its historic nature. Millions of people visit each year. The walk to the lighthouse is scenic; on the boardwalk, you will see dunes, tall beach grass, and wildlife. Be sure not to feed the wildlife, and you could be fined. They may look cute, but you are warned.

21. MONTAUK POINT

Everyone who comes to Long Island for vacation or even a day trip should make their way down to Montauk Point. This is considered "The End" of Long Island. Montauk, home the Montauk Point lighthouse and is regarded as a New York State Park. This park is 862-acres of camping, swimming, lighthouse tours, fishing, etc. The Montauk Point Lighthouse is one of the oldest lighthouses in America. It was authorized by the Second Congress under the presidency of George Washington in 1972 to be constructed. Construction began on June 7th, 1796, and finished on November 5th, 1796. Montauk has more entertainment besides the lighthouse. Since it is a state park, you can enjoy their hiking trails, shopping, restaurants, and campgrounds. Also, parts

of the beach that the lighthouse is on allows
swimming, or you can risk it and go in where there
are no lifeguards. You should only do this if you're
an experienced swimmer.

22. EATING LOCAL IN MONTAUK POINT

The Point Bar and Grill is more of a laid-back
joint. This is an environment for young adults looking
to dance the night away. The Point offers live music,
trivia nights, and Happy Hours Monday-Friday.
Come and enjoy a burger and a beer and watch sports
games on their 17 flat-screen TV. Yes, I said it, 17
large flat-screen TV's; you'll never miss a game. 668
The Gig Shack, or better known by the locals, "The
Shack, is one of the renowned downtown Montauk
restaurants. The best way to describe the food is that
it is a global surf cuisine, but it has an international
twist. Or in simpler terms, excellent, tasty, light food.
This is a family-owned business, and the head chef is
the youngest of the three sons, Gary. At the same
time, the rest of the family takes care of the front of

the restaurant. When you come into their restaurant, it is as if you are having dinner with family.

23. SHOP LOCAL: MONTAUK POINT

Montauk Mainstay is one of the most popular shops in the area. Family-owned, they offer other locations through the south fork as well. Mostly an appealing store; they have different brands of mostly local shops and restaurant brands. This family created the idea of Montauk Mainstay while fluke fishing while eating egg sandwiches. But soon, they made it a reality. Visit this store and buy their fantastic apparel. You can't leave Montauk without a "The End" shirt anyway; every tourist needs one. Another trendy and famous store is the Montauk Clothing Company. Everyone who visits needs to see the apparel they offer in this store. Even the locals shop in this store! They don't only provide souvenir clothing with "Montauk" etched into every shirt, but they offer actual clothes. For example, dresses, shorts, t-shirts, etc. Montauk Clothing Company provides clothing for all, even kids. This is another store you need to visit before heading home.

24. GREY GARDENS

Most have heard of Grey Gardens from the remake movie that cast Drew Barrymore as Little Edie Bouvier Beale and Jessica Lange as Edith Ewing Bouvier Beale. Edith and Little Edie are mother and daughter and were known as First Lady, Jackie Kennedy's aunt (Edith), and first cousin (Little Edie.) Located at 3 West End Road and Lily Pond Lane in the Georgica Pond neighborhood of East Hampton, the Beale Family owned this prestigious home from 1924 to 1979. Little Eddie and Edith only lived there from 1952-1979. Sadly, the Beale girls let the place go. The gorgeous gardens they once had were all dead plants and garbage, and the house was crumbling down around them because of the stray cats they allowed in. Edith only cared about those cats rather than her daughter. In 1975 there was a documentary made about the Beales and the fantastic home they lived in. They lived in squalor, and the documentary captured their life. It is considered one of the best documentaries of all time. A 2006 musical was made, and a movie based on the Beale girl's life and the men directing and filming the documentary.

The house dates back to 1897 and was designed by Joseph Greenleaf Thorpe. Other owners of the mansion were Ben Bradlee. He was once a prominent journalist of post-World War II America and also was the first managing editor of the Washington Post. He became a public figure once he published the Pentagon Papers and gave the go-ahead on publishing information on the Watergate Scandal. Sally Quinn also wrote for the Washington Post; Her specialty to write about is religion. They both lived together at Grey Gardens from 1979 to 2014. They improved the estate and tried to restore it to the greatness it once had. But sadly, Ben died in 2014 at 93 and was sold. Currently, Liz Lange, who is a well-known fashion designer, resides there now. The Estate is 1.1 acres, 3,516-foot home off the water with a flourishing garden. The home features five bedrooms, four full baths, a paneled carriage room with a fireplace, a shaded terrace, and balconies overlooking the water. The house also has a dining and garden room, with a two-car garage. When it was sold in 2014, it was sold for 15.5 million dollars. You can't take the odor of the home, but the outside of it is incredible. It is a piece of history that many should see, especially the beautiful restoration of the house.

25. SAGAMORE HILL

Located in Oyster Bay, New York, in Nassau County, Sagamore Hill was home to the 26th president of the United States, Theodore Roosevelt. From 1885 to his death in 1919, Roosevelt resided there with his family. His home is located in an incorporated village of Cove Neck, New York, which is a part of Oyster Bay. The little town is on a small peninsular that is roughly 2 miles. This is on the North Shore of Long Island, east of Manhattan. Today, Sagamore Hill is now a State Park, which is perfect since Roosevelt was the father of all state parks. His home and the grounds are all open for viewing and hiking. His house has a guided tour of his life on Long Island and his family. It is the most memorable tour on Long Island. As we all know, Roosevelt was a hunter; well, everything he hunted, he brought home.

Throughout Roosevelt's childhood, he had spent time in Oyster Bay with his family, but at the age of 22, he purchased his land. He owned 155 arcs of land for $30,000. That was a lot of money in 1880. That equals out in today's economy at $794,793. The

North room, which is the most impressive room on tour, has trophies from former president's hunts, gifts from foreign dignitaries, alongside pieces of art and books from the Roosevelts' collection. This tour opens your eyes to what kind of a man he was. The time includes 23 other rooms in the house.

26. OHEKA CASTLE

Oheka, also known as the Otto Kahn Estate, is a luxurious hotel located on the north shore of Long Island in West Hills, New York. West Hills is a hamlet in the town of Huntington, New York. This beautiful estate was once the home of Otto Hermann Kahn and his family. The castle got its nickname, Oheka, using an acronym using the first several letters of each part of its creator's name: Otto Herman Kahn. Kahn built the mansion in between 1914 and 1919. Oheka is the second-largest privet home in America. The castle has 127 rooms and is 109,000 square feet. Today, Oheka is a historic hotel with 32 guest rooms and suites. Its most popular use is for weddings. The castle has been the backdrop of many movies, tv shows, and music videos. The castle also has a bar, restaurant, mansion tours, and beautiful gardens. In 2004 the estate was listed on the National Register of Historic Places. This castle needs a visit. If you can't stay in the hotel, you need to take the mansion tour to see the most beautiful places on Long Island.

27. OLD WESTBURY GARDENS

Old Westbury Gardens was once the home of a businessman, John Shaffer Phipps. The gardens and estate are located at 71 Old Westbury Road in Old Westbury. In 1959, a year after Shaffer died, it became a museum home. It is open for tours from April through October. In 1903, the construction started on the estate after he promised his fiancé, Margarita Grace, that he would build a home that was a republic of her family's British residence located in Battle, East Sussex, England. The estate was finished in 1906 for his now wife and children. The house was designed by a British designer George A. Crawley; he was assisted by an American architect Grosvenor Atterbury. The home consists of 23 rooms, and the grounds cover 160 arcs. Between the garden and estate tours, you will see some gorgeous sights. They also have many events going on all year round, such as fairs and workshops about backyard learning and discovery.

28. RISE OF THE JACK O' LANTERNS

The Rise of the Jack o' lanterns has to be one of the most popular events during the fall on Long Island. People from near and far travel just to see this unique holiday event.   The Rise of the Jack o' Lantern is most of October for Halloween. There are 5,000 hand-carved illuminated pumpkins. They are creatively placed along a path set to music. Everyone needs to experience the Rise of the Jack o' Lantern, but be sure to get your tickets in advance. They sell out quickly.

29. PLANTING FIELDS ARBORETUM

Planting fields are one of the unique state parks on Long Island. This is not a park where you can play sports or picnic. This is a park where the gardens and admiration work hard to provide a scenic, relaxing experience. Planting Fields is for its scenic paths and plants. They have greenhouses that they decorate for the season, Coe Hall, a historic home where the Coe Family resided, and they have a bunch of family-friendly events. They are sure to have visitors all year round because they decorate the park for each holiday and season and have events. For example, Arbor Day, The Holiday Tree Lighting, different exhibits, yoga events, etc.

30. COLE HALL HOUSE MUSEUM

Coe Hall Historic House Museum is located within the Planting Fields Arboretum State Historic Park. The park is located in Oyster Bay, New York, no too far away from Sagamore Hill. Cole Hall was once the home of William Robertson Coe, an insurance and railroad executive, and his wife Mary Huttleston Coe lived in the house from 1913 until 1918 when it burned to the ground. Coe did build a grander house that stands today. This home was also designed in

1906 by the American architect, Grosvenor Atterbury, but it was initially for James Byrne, a New York City Lawyer. He eventually sold it to William Robertson Coe in 1913. Coe is an English immigrant who came over to Ellis Island with his ten brothers and sisters in 1883. At the age of 15, he landed himself an office boy job at a maritime insurer, which was absorbed by Johnson and Higgins Insurance Company of New York. As time went on, Cole became the President of Johnson and Higgins in 1916. Cole married three times. The first time, his wife died unexpectedly in 1898; they were only married for five years. The second, Mary Coe, married for 24 years and her father, who was also in the insurance business, boosted Coe's insurance career. Mary died at the age of 49 at Planting Fields. Mr. Coe then married a divorcee named Caroline Graham Slaughter.

Coe Hall is one of the most beautiful museum houses on the Island. Mostly constructed in stone, it grand and houses the most beautiful antique furniture. There are tours that you can take to learn more about the years that the Coe's lived in the estate and also how Planting Fields became one of the historic state parks and museum houses. During the holiday events, like the holiday tree lighting, they allow visitors inside the house to guide themselves through the open rooms. There is a small café, so you won't have to leave for lunch just to come back to finish enjoying the sights. There is a small gift shop as well to bring goodies home to your family and friends.

31. OLD BETHPAGE RESTORATION VILLAGE

Old Bethpage Restoration Village is more than just a collection of historic houses; there is a knowledgeable, dedicated, and talented staff that are in character the whole duration of being on the grounds of the village. They are the ones that bring the entire historic town to life. People who visit walk back in time to the 1860s; this was the civil war in America. Depending on the season, they dress up the village for the upcoming holidays. For Christmas, they offer a lantern walk where you bring your lantern, of course, a candle, do not get a battery-operated lantern, remember it's the 1860's. The walk is at night, which the lantern you'll be grateful for. When they say the village goes back in time to the 1860s, they think of every little detail, including the lights. They have events going on during the lantern walk like bonfires, apple cider, and desserts available. The actors make any of the food that you eat on the premise. They do this with equipment that they would have used in the 1860s. During the summer, you can catch a baseball game, play with the actor children with the toys of the time, visit the houses of different families in the village where you can learn about each of their jobs around the house and farms. There is livestock that the actors work with throughout the town. It is very well done, family-oriented activities are available. This is something that you don't find everywhere, there are only a few places that do it correctly, and Bethpage is one of them. You can buy tickets in advance for this attraction. So instead of waiting on line, you can purchase them online and just walk in. I know if you go on the weekend, it will be busy, but they have more activities, especially for the kids during the weekends.

32. CEDAR BEACH

Okay, beach, mostly a little gated community of beach homes owned and rented out by some locals. You can have a lot of fun on Cedar Beach; This beach is located on Fire Island, but you can access it while driving to Jonas beach. There is a lot of fun to be had here. After a day of laying on the beach, you can head over to the Salt Shack that has an outdoor theater and outdoor bar. They have your classic drinks and the famous Long Island Iced Tea. The best band that plays there is That 70s Band. They play all the classics music of the 70s. They will have you out of your seat, drink in hand, dancing the night away. When you're in town, check out their Facebook Page or website; they always keep everyone posted on where they will be.

33. ISLIP

Islip is a tiny town that, while driving through it, you probably won't even know you're in Islip. This is also my hometown. I have lived in Islip most of my life, and I can say there is plenty to do. The restaurants and bars are always good to go too; they have live music and outdoor seating. From the bars on Main Street, you can take an evening walk towards Islip beach, which looks out to the bay. From there, you can see the Robert Moses Bridge and the Fire Island Lighthouse. There is also an eatery and bar on the beach. We also have little boutiques and jewelry shops.

34. LONG IRELAND

Long Ireland is one of the most popular breweries on the Island. The Brewery opened in 2009 by Dan Burke and Greg Martin, two ordinary guys who quit their day jobs and started making beer. They have their taproom where you can see the tanks they use to brew the beer. They are open seven days a week and offer flights and a beer garden with lawn games. You can also bring along your furry friends, indoor and outdoor! They always have events going on, all year round, and every night something is going on. For example, one of the nights during the week, they play records featured by the staff. Anyone around to drink can look through the box of vinyl they have and play them. Their beet is smooth and tasty too. They have so many options that won't disappoint.

35. TRANSPORTATION

The one thing about Long Island is, you need a car to get around. Everyone knows in New York City you don't have to bring your vehicle with you, saving you stress and money. But on Long Island, it is very much needed. There are busses if you are willing to ride along those, but they don't come as often as city busses do. Another source of transportation is the Long Island railroad. But to get from the point of Long Island to Queens and everything in-between, you should have a car. There are rentals locations everywhere if you need to fly in.

36. NASSAU COLISEUM

They are also known as the Nassau Veterans Memorial Coliseum, is located in Uniondale, New York. It is a multipurpose indoor arena for sports and concerts. The event showcases the circus when it comes to town. The Nassau Coliseum was home to the New York Islanders Hockey Team before moving to the Berkley Center in Brooklyn. It was also home to the New York Net, but they also moved to the Barkley Center. The Nassau Coliseum is mostly used for music events and wrestling WWE Smackdown.

37. HIKING TRAILS ON EASTERN LONG ISLAND

The popularity of the eastern part of the island is not the little towns on boutiques and mom and pop eateries, but the scenery. The forks are probably the most beautiful places on the island. And with all this natural beauty comes hikers from all around the world to walk along our trails. Inlet Pound County Park is located in Southold, New York. It is a 1.5-mile walk through hardwood forest and maritime wood that leads to a freshwater pond and the Long Island Sound. Long Island Pine Barrens Trail is another popular trail for avid hikers. As the nation's second-largest pine barrens through a 47-mile route, you may want to leave this to the professionals. The course goes from Rocky Point, New York, to the Shinnecock Canal.

Mashomack Preserve Hiking trail in Shelter Island is a 2,039-acre preserve that has something for every hiker. There are 1.5 miles, 3-6 miles, and a 10-mile loop of trails that snake through the oak-hickory forest, across open fields and beside pounds and marches. Of course, Montauk point offers the most outstanding trails on the point of Long Island. These trails provide stunning views of the ocean and where Block Island means the sound. From November to April, you can watch seals sun on the rocks offshore.

38. HIKING ON WESTERN LONG ISLAND

Cold Spring Harbor State Park is located in Nassau County, not too far from Oheka Castle; on the trails, you'll be able to sneak peeks at the castle from afar. The hiking trail runs a total of 5.4 miles, with 40 acres to explore. You can also see the Hewitt House that was built in 1815. Another Western State Park you can visit that offers hiking is Trail View, State Park. The trail is 6.9 miles, which should only take 3 hours. There are over 400 acres of land that borders Cold Spring Harbor State Park and Bethpage State Park, which means you could spend a day or more exploring the hiking in Nassau County. There isn't much hiking on the West end of the island because as you get closer to the city, everything starts to get pushed together. But these two state parks are needed to see when visiting Long Island.

39. SUFFOLK THEATER

The Suffolk Theater is small in the middle of Riverhead's Main Street. It offers musical events like tribute bands, and sometimes you can get some big names like Three Dog Night. They also have comedy shows and holiday-themed events as well. This is a smaller venue than something like the Nassau Coliseum. It is also cheaper too; if you want to have a night of entertainment, but don't want to spend a lot of money, go to the Suffolk Theater.

40. LIRR

The Long Island Railroad is another form of transportation to get to places throughout Long Island. 11 lines can get you to where you need to be. You can get from Penn Station to Montauk Point. You'll only have to switch trains once at Babylon. It is still smart to have a car, but if the destination isn't far from the train station, then go ahead, check out the Long Island Railroad. Also, if you buy tickets, they are suitable for six months. And the LIRR offers online ticket purchases. This is good if you are running late; you can buy them right on your phone.

41. CANOES/KAYAK RENTALS

If you are an adventurer and love to canoe or kayak, here are a few places where you can rent the boats and set sail from. If you are out towards Nassau, one of the best places to go to is Atlantic Outfitters in Port Washington. They offer paddle boats for kids, rowboats, canoe rentals, and more. You'll set sail on the Manhasset Bay on the North Shore of Long Island. Another boat rental shop if you are closer to the eastern part of Long Island is in Smithtown, Blydenburgh County Park. This is a 627-acre park that offers Stump Pond. It is renowned as one of the most picturesque on Long Island. You can visit Memorial Day to Labor Day and enjoy your day on a rowboat or a canoe. They also offer camping, picnicking, birdwatching, and fishing.

42. SHOPPING MALLS

There are a few indoor shopping malls that you can spend a lazy day searching for some deals. The mall that has the most to offer is the Smith Haven Mall; located in Lake Grove, New York, this mall has many designer shops like Hollister, Abercrombie and Fitch, Michael Kors, etc. They have a few popular restaurants like Bobby's Burger Palace, Bobby Flay's Burger joint. Or you can head over to California Pizza Kitchen or The Cheesecake Factory. All have excellent food, great options, and indoor and outdoor dining.

43. TANGER OUTLET SHOPPING CENTERS

There are only two Tanger Outlet Shopping Centers on the Island, Deer Park or Riverhead. Both have fantastic designer stores at department store prices—everyone who are locals on the island shop at these outlets. Their prices are way lower than the actual stores. For example, Michael Kors, they are always having between 50%-70% off bags. When you go to Michael Kors in the mall, everything is at a retail price. They also have dining on campus and parking. These places become incredibly packed, especially during the holidays.

44. LONG ISLAND SEASONS

Now, Long Island is an island, but we have four seasons. Summers can be brutal on the island. The humidity will have you running towards the shoreline or staying in the air conditioning. It can become unbearable at times. But luckily, we do have beaches on all sides of the island, so you are never far from relief. The Fall is probably the best time of the year to come to long island. The humidity is gone, and it is chilly out. Also, the color of the leaves change color, and it is one of the most beautiful views of the island, especially on the eastern part of the island where there are more wooded areas. Winters are harsh. There are winters where we get snow almost every day, then there are other winters where we see nothing, it is a gamble, but it is cold. We have had a few freeze out days where the town officials have said to wear something to protect our faces from the cold. Spring is fantastic in New York. The flowers start to bloom; the island becomes green again, not cold or too hot. You can pull off a light jacket on most days.

45. PORT JEFFERSON

Port Jefferson is a North Shore village off the sound. It is a little town with excellent restaurants, shopping, and the Bridgeport, Connecticut Ferry. Suppose you are interested in hopping a ferry to visit some casinos or visit other parts of New England, instead of driving through New York City and around the horn. This saves time and money. There are cute older homes all over the hills of Port Jefferson. The architecture of these homes is a must-see; many owners try to keep it as original as possible. You can also walk the boardwalk with ice cream from the most significant family-owned ice cream and candy shop in Rogers Frigate. A lot of their candy, ice cream, and desserts are homemade and excellent. This is a must-visit while visiting Long Island.

46. BABYLON VILLAGE

Suppose you are looking for a village where you can party until the sun comes up, head to Babylon Village. There are 50 plus locations to find a great drink and great food. A lot of these places also offer live music, trivia nights, and DJ dance parties. The parking isn't ample in Babylon, but the train station is right in town. Depending on where you are staying, you can take the train into Babylon and enjoy the night without worry about driving or if you need to feed the meter.

47. FLUX COFFEE

I know New York is home of the Starbucks and Dunkin Donut shops, but if you want a unique place to grab a decent size cup of jo without breaking the bank, get over flux coffee in Farmingdale, New York. They give you this container that looks like Tupperware, which is called Flux Coffee: Big Ass Drink! From there, they mark off what you want in your coffee and what type of coffee and hand it over to the barista to make it. You can buy their coffee, merch, and grinders. They even offer pastries and sandwiches! This pace is a unique coffee shop that everyone raves about.

48. SUNKEN MEADOW BEACH

Sunken Meadow State Park and Beach are one of the prettiest beaches on the Northside of Long Island. There isn't a mean due to the rocks. The part is open year-round from sunrise to sunset and has 3 miles of just beach and a boardwalk that is 6 miles. They offer horseback riding and bike riding as well. There is also a golf course that features 27 holes that could be played in 9 or 18 holes. The course was built in 1962. They offer hiking trails and have a pavilion for weddings and other events. The sand isn't as rocky as the other beaches on the northside and overlooks the sound.

49. HUNTINGTON VILLAGE

Huntington Village is a small town on the northern side of Long Island; it is a little quaint and quiet town. Along New York Ave, you can find a few stand out stores like Michells; this a family-owned business of a well-known Connecticut and Huntington Family. They opened in 1958 and were founded by Ed and Norma Michells with three men's suits, a coffee pot, and a dream. Soon came along their sons, Bill and Jack, in the 1960s. They specialize in women's and men's clothing, jewelry, and accessories. After all the hard work this family has put into this business, they have a lot to show for it. Michells has 9 locations between the east coast and west coast.

50. EAT LOCAL IN HUNTINGTON VILLAGE

Along New York Ave, you can access shops, restaurants, and coffee locations. They have some of the best restaurants on the island. Albert's, which is an Asian Fusion restaurant, is one of the popular places to spend a Friday or Saturday night. Their food is fantastic, and they offer to take out! Another great place to visit for brunch is The Shed. This place is always full, so be sure to make a reservation or get there early

BONUS TIP 1:   THE VANDERBILT ESTATE MUSEUM

The Vanderbilt Museum is located in Centerport, Long Island, close Huntington Village. This estate is on 44 acres and named for William Vanderbilt. The estate has 24 rooms of Spanish design. It was created by a famed New York architecture firm Warren and Wetmore, which designed and built Grand Central Terminal. They offer guided tours around the estate as well as a planetarium that opened in 1971. This is another historical site to visit on Long Island. It is a one of a kind out of all the estates the Vanderbilt's used to own on Long Island.

BONUS TIP 2:   CRAZY BEANS

Located in Stoney Brook, New York, Crazy Beans is an unusual restaurant and coffee shop. Crazy Beans motto stands out to people who don't always fit in or are maybe a rebel in their way; They believe that people who are crazy enough to think they can change the world will end up being the ones that do. That is an impressive outlook on life. This place is

fun, wacky, and has fantastic food and coffee. Their
menus consist of breakfast, lunch, and out of this
world drink concoctions that are not just coffee.

BONUS TIP 3: RIVERHEAD AQUARIUM

The Riverhead aquarium may be a little pricy, but
it worth it. They offer indoor exhibits like the
Amazon Rainforest, Butterflies, Birds, and views of
Coral Reef. The outdoor displays are fun, especially
the fantastic show the sea lions put on for their guests.
You can also visit the animals that the aquarium
recently has been rescued and being rehabilitated.
There is much more to see in the Long Island
Aquarium; you should visit.

BONUS TIP 4: SPLISH SPLASH WATER PARK

If you are looking to take the kids for some fun
during the summer, take them to Splish Splash. This
is an outdoor water park located in Riverhead, New

York. They have water rides and pools to beat the humidity of a New York Summer. It sits on 96 acres of family-friendly fun, including 20 water slides, rides, and attractions, like live-action shows. They have family dining from Johnny Rockets, gift shops, and a large picnic area. They offer accommodations for larger parties, like reunions or school field trips

BONUS TIP 5: ADVENTURELAND

If you are a fan of amusement parks, visit Adventureland! Located in Farmingdale, New York, Adventureland has been Long Island's leading amusement park since 1962. There is a total of 32 rides, two of which are roller-coaster. This isn't as big as a Six Flags, but it is useful if you have smaller children. Adventureland is a seasonal business; they are not open in the winter months. They have restaurants, arcades, and little gift shops to bring home goodies for the family. This is a great place to get your family for a cheap and comfortable day of fun.

PACKING AND PLANNING TIPS

A Week before Leaving

- Arrange for someone to take care of pets and water plants.

- Email and Print important Documents.

- Get Visa and vaccines if needed.

- Check for travel warnings.

- Stop mail and newspaper.

- Notify Credit Card companies where you are going.

- Passports and photo identification is up to date.

- Pay bills.

- Copy important items and download travel Apps.

- Start collecting small bills for tips.

- Have post office hold mail while you are away.

- Check weather for the week.

- Car inspected, oil is changed, and tires have the correct pressure.

- Check airline luggage restrictions.

- Download Apps needed for your trip.

Right Before Leaving

- Contact bank and credit cards to tell them your location.

- Clean out refrigerator.

- Empty garbage cans.

- Lock windows.

- Make sure you have the proper identification with you.

- Bring cash for tips.

- Remember travel documents.

- Lock door behind you.

- Remember wallet.

- Unplug items in house and pack chargers.

- Change your thermostat settings.

- Charge electronics, and prepare camera memory cards.

READ OTHER GREATER THAN A TOURIST BOOKS

Greater Than a Tourist- Geneva Switzerland: 50 Travel Tips from a Local by Amalia Kartika

Greater Than a Tourist- St. Croix US Birgin Islands USA: 50 Travel Tips from a Local by Tracy Birdsall

Greater Than a Tourist- San Juan Puerto Rico: 50 Travel Tips from a Local by Melissa Tait

Greater Than a Tourist – Lake George Area New York USA: 50 Travel Tips from a Local by Janine Hirschklau

Greater Than a Tourist – Monterey California United States: 50 Travel Tips from a Local by Katie Begley

Greater Than a Tourist – Chanai Crete Greece: 50 Travel Tips from a Local by Dimitra Papagrigoraki

Greater Than a Tourist – The Garden Route Western Cape Province South Africa: 50 Travel Tips from a Local by Li-Anne McGregor van Aardt

Greater Than a Tourist – Sevilla Andalusia Spain: 50 Travel Tips from a Local by Gabi Gazon

Children's Book: *Charlie the Cavalier Travels the World* by Lisa Rusczyk Ed. D.

> TOURIST

Follow us on Instagram for beautiful travel images:
http://Instagram.com/GreaterThanATourist

Follow *Greater Than a Tourist* on Amazon.

>Tourist Podcast

>T Website

>T Youtube

>T Facebook

>T Goodreads

>T Amazon

>T Mailing List

>T Pinterest

>T Instagram

>T Twitter

>T SoundCloud

>T LinkedIn

>T Map

> TOURIST

At *Greater Than a Tourist*, we love to share travel tips with you. How did we do? What guidance do you have for how we can give you better advice for your next trip? Please send your feedback to GreaterThanaTourist@gmail.com as we continue to improve the series. We appreciate your constructive feedback. Thank you.

METRIC CONVERSIONS

TEMPERATURE

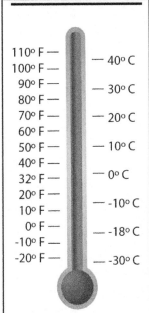

110° F —   — 40° C
100° F —
90° F —   — 30° C
80° F —
70° F —   — 20° C
60° F —
50° F —   — 10° C
40° F —
32° F —   — 0° C
20° F —
10° F —   — -10° C
0° F —
-10° F —   — -18° C
-20° F —   — -30° C

To convert F to C:

Subtract 32, and then multiply by 5/9 or .5555.

To Convert C to F:

Multiply by 1.8 and then add 32.

32F = 0C

LIQUID VOLUME

To Convert:....................Multiply by
U.S. Gallons to Liters................ 3.8
U.S. Liters to Gallons 26
Imperial Gallons to U.S. Gallons 1.2
Imperial Gallons to Liters....... 4.55
Liters to Imperial Gallons 22
1 Liter = .26 U.S. Gallon
1 U.S. Gallon = 3.8 Liters

DISTANCE

To convert ....Multiply by
Inches to Centimeters 2.54
Centimeters to Inches 39
Feet to Meters...................... .3
Meters to Feet 3.28
Yards to Meters 91
Meters to Yards 1.09
Miles to Kilometers 1.61
Kilometers to Miles............ .62
1 Mile = 1.6 km
1 km = .62 Miles

WEIGHT

1 Ounce = .28 Grams
1 Pound = .4555 Kilograms
1 Gram = .04 Ounce
1 Kilogram = 2.2 Pounds

TRAVEL QUESTIONS

- Do you bring presents home to family or friends after a vacation?

- Do you get motion sick?

- Do you have a favorite billboard?

- Do you know what to do if there is a flat tire?

- Do you like a sun roof open?

- Do you like to eat in the car?

- Do you like to wear sun glasses in the car?

- Do you like toppings on your ice cream?

- Do you use public bathrooms?

- Did you bring a cell phone and does it have power?

- Do you have a form of identification with you?

- Have you ever been pulled over by a cop?

- Have you ever given money to a stranger on a road trip?

- Have you ever taken a road trip with animals?

- Have you ever gone on a vacation alone?

- Have you ever run out of gas?

- If you could move to any place in the world, where would it be?

- If you could travel anywhere in the world, where would you travel?

- If you could travel in any vehicle, which one would it be?

- If you had three things to wish for from a magic genie, what would they be?

- If you have a driver's license, how many times did it take you to pass the test?

- What are you the most afraid of on vacation?

- What do you want to get away from the most when you are on vacation?

- What foods smell bad to you?

- What item do you bring on ever trip with you away from home?

- What makes you sleepy?

- What song would you love to hear on the radio when you're cruising on the highway?

- What travel job would you want the least?

- What will you miss most while you are away from home?

- What is something you always wanted to try?

- What is the best road side attraction that you ever saw?

- What is the farthest distance you ever biked?

- What is the farthest distance you ever walked?

- What is the weirdest thing you needed to buy while on vacation?

- What is your favorite candy?

- What is your favorite color car?

- What is your favorite family vacation?

- What is your favorite food?

- What is your favorite gas station drink or food?

- What is your favorite license plate design?

- What is your favorite restaurant?

- What is your favorite smell?

- What is your favorite song?

- What is your favorite sound that nature makes?

- What is your favorite thing to bring home from a vacation?

- What is your favorite vacation with friends?

- What is your favorite way to relax?

- Where is the farthest place you ever traveled in a car?

- Where is the farthest place you ever went North, South, East and West?

- Where is your favorite place in the world?

- Who is your favorite singer?

- Who taught you how to drive?

- Who will you miss the most while you are away?

- Who if the first person you will contact when you get to your destination?

- Who brought you on your first vacation?

- Who likes to travel the most in your life?

- Would you rather be hot or cold?

- Would you rather drive above, below, or at the speed limited?

- Would you rather drive on a highway or a back road?

- Would you rather go on a train or a boat?

- Would you rather go to the beach or the woods?

TRAVEL BUCKET LIST

1.

2.

3.

4.

5.

6.

7.

8.

9.

10.

Printed in Great Britain
by Amazon

34919647R00056